MW00811138

UNDRESSING
THE WORLD

poems by

Kathy Kremin [signature]

Kathy Kremins

Finishing Line Press
Georgetown, Kentucky

UNDRESSING
THE WORLD

Copyright © 2022 by Kathy Kremins
ISBN 978-1-64662-860-5 First Edition
All rights reserved under International and Pan-American Copyright Conventions.
No part of this book may be reproduced in any manner whatsoever without written
permission from the publisher, except in the case of brief quotations embodied in
critical articles and reviews.

ACKNOWLEDGMENTS

"Church Raffle" was originally published in *Paterson Literary Review*, Issue
27
"My Mother's Hands" was originally published in *Paterson Literary Review*,
Issue 50

Publisher: Leah Huete de Maines
Editor: Christen Kincaid
Cover Art: Marina Carreira
Author Photo: Ysabel Y. Gonzalez
Cover Design: Elizabeth Maines McCleavy

Order online: www.finishinglinepress.com
also available on amazon.com

Author inquiries and mail orders:
Finishing Line Press
PO Box 1626
Georgetown, Kentucky 40324
USA

Table of Contents

*The best people are the ones you have to forgive
for everything. You have no choice;
it would've been worse to live without them.*
Elizabeth Wurtzel

My Mother's Hands

Those hands, eighty-seven years of history imprinted on callused
fingertips and broad palms that my bottom knows too well,
blue-purple veins coursing a map of work, motherhood, and love
in all that you've touched:
cutting turf in the bogs of Roscommon;
signing your name in a pained scrawl
in the Ellis Island logbook; caressing
the strong thigh of the only man
you ever loved; testing TV tubes
in the slate gray Newark factory;
bathing my tiny body with hard
hands gone soft with mother-love;
slicing meat for the sandwiches
in the college cafeteria, all the education
you ever needed, you said.

You came home one day
from church to find Dad,
still, breath-less,
lying on the couch,
your hands moving over forehead
across cheeks and closed eyes,
memorizing his face,
resting your head where
his once beating heart lay
quiet, filled with profound silence.

How does grief become so small
it can be carried
in the palm of one's hand?

Mass

Learning to pray
in your way,
steady on the kneeler
upright, no butt
on the seat,
fraught with distraction.
The priest in bright
red robes edged in gilded
gold embroidery
and the altar boy swinging
incense took me places
that if you knew I went
would have elicited spanking.
Replacing the dirge-like
hymns, the priest, the boy
and I became part of a morality
play resembling a Broadway
musical, and I would rearrange
the church into my own theater.

Ghosts

I.

Lying on the living room floor,
counting tiles on the ceiling—
there were twenty-one—
I waited for Casper
the Friendly Ghost, my hero,
kind, gentle, smart,
anticipating his theme song,
I saw a man in a dark hat stick his hand
toward a man in an undershirt like my father's.
Bang!

II.

It is November 24, 1963, and someone
died. Two days before, President Kennedy
was shot. My mother ran from Thom McCann's
before I got my Keds and dragged me home
past crying, angry people on Orange Street.

The house was so silent
those few days and most of my cartoons
interrupted or canceled, I figured
by November 24, my shows would return.
On our black and white Magnavox,
Bugs and Donald lived in a Technicolor
imagination, a cast of friends
I could depend on every day.
Then everything changed.

Now a place where the dead vanished
on the screen. The undershirt guy grabbed
his stomach and pain flipped across his face.
This Lee Harvey had been shot and the picture

became scrambled and blacked out.
It was still November 24, 1963
and someone else would die.

III.

Casper couldn't rescue my eyes.
He was locked inside the TV
behind all the dying
and I laid down again except this time
my face was buried in the rug away
from the ceiling.
I had forgotten how to count.

War Dreams

Okinawa seemed safe
to me, so soft in my mouth,

a cotton-candy lace
with hot sun and palm trees

and tropical beaches,
unlike the hard hammer

and blood taste of Vietnam.
So why was everyone crying?

Hugs that pressed faces into necks,
kissing Cousin Bucky good-bye,

faces into chests, chests to chests
with slaps on the back,

handshake semi-hug chest bumps
and the full-body sag of lovers

holding each other up.
My father, WWII gunners mate,

wiped away tears in a gesture as angry
as his voice saying if he had a son

he would send him to Canada.
I knew the war was in Vietnam,

I had seen the helicopters,
the men with guns in the jungles,

my father's face as the body bags
were flown out.

Vietnam in my dreams
where my friends were soldiers

walking around without limbs
and bullets flew from their mouths

killing children that looked like me.
Yet I still played Army

in the thin alleyways of 4th Street
between the two-family houses

and we all died a few times a day.
I didn't know that in Canada

a boy could stay alive
and be called a traitor

because he didn't want to die.

Cemetery

I.

On Saturdays,
you spoke slowly and carefully
and you smelled funny.
A sweet, fermenting smell
with a hint of vomit.
Talking vigorously and intimately
to the hibiscus, dirt matted
into your hands,
you sucked its scent deep
into your gardener's blood.
During school,
when I heard sirens,
I was sure it was you
in that ambulance,
lying so still on the stretcher.
You had another heart attack
or you were in a car accident
or you had too much to drink,
had fallen and hit your head.
Often, when I did get to the car outside school,
you were asleep and I had to wake you.
The smell of sweet brandy and puke
clung to everything;
slumped in the driver's seat,
the earth falls away.
You stumble out of the car,
reach for me, a puny stalk
defying the seasons.
Bending with the weight,
I plant you in the car,
crying and running home to Mom,
seeing your frozen and withered body.

Mom abruptly appears:
your father's sick, she says.

II.

I imagine you in the yard
with your plants and vegetables.
In your jeans, hanging low in front
and faded at the knees
from tending to your garden with meticulous care;
tools laid out on a cloth,
surgeon's instruments in your hands,
cleaning the area and turning the soil,
preparing for the planting
humming and whistling bird songs;
a white undershirt, damp with perspiration;
small, stubby-fingered hands with the earth
packed under the nails;
and your bald head,
a horseshoe of hair outlining it,
protected by the blue and orange Mets cap.
You and Ron Swoboda were my heroes,
diving and making one-hand catches
at Shea and in the backyard,
saving the game in the bottom of the ninth.
Each season brought different smells
and you carried them home
on your hands, jeans, jacket.
Winter was my favorite:
balsam, pine, evergreen
mixed with the spiced apple breath of cider.
That is where I see you.
Red Santa hat and vest,
quarters handed out to visiting children,
not owning your own home

until you were sixty-two and finding out,
when you applied for a mortgage,
you had no credit because all your life
you paid in cash.
And you, carrying Aunt Mary,
up and downstairs for two years
while she slowly died.
You said,
she needs to be with people
and out in the yard
because that is where life is.

III.

I visited the Empire State Building
the day you died.
Far from the grit of the earth
and the blossoming daffodils,
my body suspended in air, temporarily.
You laid down on the couch
with Barney, our dog.
That's how Mom found you.
That afternoon you got your garden ready.
And every spring as I kneel
in black soil with tender plants
digging a home for the roots,
my hands are in your hands,
working in the earth
to create neat rows of peonies,
gladiolas, pansies, hyacinth
and daffodils, bee heaven.
As you always said,
when it is time to go,
I'll go quietly from home
with all my flowers in order.

On Burning
(Roseville)

It is September of my sixth-grade year and the highway is coming and vacant lots where houses, somebody's home, turn our block into a jumble of broken glass, dangerous to the touch, razor-sharp and smelling like Pabst and gardens of tires set on fire by teenagers.

Bought out by the state, her home for twenty years, Mrs. Cannon's house with its grease spattered kitchen, bedroom ceiling marked with circles of smoke from her husband's cigarettes, screened-in porch where her two sons played bicycle gladiators, its wooden walls cut and gouged, last week was plowed into a heap of wood.

We stand in the streets in the early morning lit up by the sparks as the firemen water down the roof of our house and the few others that still remain while little pieces of fire jump through the air, my home saved, in this neighborhood where sparks are flying and buildings are crumbling to ash and my mother expects me to go to school after another night of burning.

Shattered Sleep

Montgomery, Mobile, Memphis,
appear in my dreams
haunt my whiteness.
Hundreds of black children's hearts
burn in their open chests, bodies lined
along the curb as the Fourth of July
parade marches past them
and white kids toss firecrackers
and white parents beam and wave
at black parents weeping
over the charred torsos of their babies.

Who is that girl wearing a white robe,
burning a cross on the Braxton's lawn?
Our neighbors, playmates, Daddy Braxton,
a World War II vet sharing a beer with Dad
over the fence in the backyard.
Memphis was a revolution started or stopped
as Dr. King fell to the floor.
Who is that white girl,
kicking the fallen King
in the face and spitting in his eyes?
She is holding the loaded gun.

Peace ain't easy, Daddy Braxton said.
Is that why I resist falling asleep?

Gallucci's Lemon Ice

We prayed in school that Mrs. Kennedy
wouldn't lose another son,
even though we didn't know her
and hadn't Mrs. King lost a son, too?
I guess we didn't pray for her
because Catholic prayers
don't mean anything to Baptist people.
Theresa and I got our change out for lemon ice
excited that Mr. Gallucci had just opened the stand.
Sitting in a darkened booth with his ear
to a transistor radio, Mr. Gallucci solemnly announced
that *Robert was dead and Ethel a widow*
with so many children what would she do?
We didn't ask for lemon ice that day
when so many people were sad
and mothers kept losing sons.
I did pray that night
for Mrs. Kennedy and Mrs. King
and all the moms of soldiers in Vietnam.
I prayed Catholic and hoped
God could translate to the Baptists, Muslims,
Lutherans, Presbyterians, Jews, Hindus,
even to moms who didn't believe in Him.
I knelt for a long time, face bent
into my hands resting on the bed.
I prayed hard,
so loud in my head
God had no choice but to hear.

"The Creator Will Provide for Us"

My first wake was Italian.
The Luciano's lost a son in Vietnam
and, at seven, the black veils and wailing
frightened and froze me so
that my mother carried me to the casket,
closed because—now I know—
of what bombs can do.

The last wake was reading yesterday's newspaper,
my closed eyes and sighing,
a silent scream for a world
that has become an open coffin
and no one to carry me away.

Aunt Mary

Your sisters still don't talk
about the cause of death.
In a family of secrets,
your death is secretive.
Always small and fragile,
an old maid,
you withered away
like a water-logged carnation
from the inside out.

I watched you
die for twenty years.
The bottle of Sangria hidden
in the attic behind the boxes
of unused shoes was yours.
The window faced east
toward the Pabst Brewery,
and its gigantic advertising bottle.

Nights of toasts to the factory
and countless bolts fitted
onto machinery you didn't understand
and nights on the pullout couch alone.

Those evenings facing east
with a glass smuggled from the kitchen,
raised in a salute
to the dreams that brought you here
on that boat from Ireland
to an attic high above Newark.
the moon uncircling through the wine
into crystals of red and urgent longing

Church Raffle

We were the only ones
in the neighborhood to ever win a car.
You played the church raffle for years
as an obligation to the Sacred Heart,
so long, in fact, you forgot
that winning was a possibility.
You were simply hoping God would remember you
when you got to the Gate—
"Oh! You're Johnny! Well, I see you always
bought a raffle ticket."
You figured any positive deed
would help your chances.

The dark green Oldsmobile
was your just reward on earth.
Waxed weekly with shined chrome,
it was a sign of wealth we didn't have.
But we could pretend as you took us
for rides through Branch Brook Park,
moving as slowly as you could get away with,
allowing time to be admired.
And us kids, tumbling in the wide back seat,
would settle down and prepare ourselves for the tunnel,
the Tunnel of Love you said,
when you and Mom kissed and then we had our turns,
kissing each of you eagerly
before returning to the rough and fearless play
that usually left satisfying welts and bruises
worn like warrior tattoos.

That Sunday morning seven years later,
you stood on the front porch
like Gatsby gazing at the green light
across the bay,
dressed for church, complete with hat,
but without a car.

You swore you parked across the street
in front of the Murphy's, under the streetlight,
but it wasn't there.
You walked up and down Alexander Street,
just in case you forgot
since you had a few beers at Cryan's on Saturday afternoon
on your way home from work.

The car was gone, though, stolen.
The cops said to *chalk it up.*
Chances were the chop shop
already divvied up the prize,
so just send in the insurance claim.
You sat on that porch all afternoon
in your church suit, hat off,
scratching and rubbing your bald head
almost like a crystal ball, making some wish.

By dinner you recovered,
teasing Mom, telling stories
and spinning philosophies.
"Easy come, easy go," you said,
assuming that God gives
and He takes away,
but I'm still wondering
what hint at judgment did He give you
by taking that graceful Oldsmobile
and replacing it with that oil slick of a Chevy Vega.
I've always worried about your entrance into Heaven
and God's sense of humor.

Whiskey-Fired

You always held my hand tightly
a reflex, for both our protection;
I fell in love with poems recited nightly,
reading under the covers until you came home.
A rocking in your step and a sparkle in your eye
as you sat on the bedside to read or sing,
it never occurred to me you were a lie,

or that you were the one with the broken wing.
Conjured from a place I thought was magic,
an elfin blue bird adopted by a big brown dog,
saved from the evil family cat—almost tragic—
is just another whiskey-fired story set in the bog.

If the crack in things lets the light in,
doesn't it also shine the dark
of where you've been?

red sweater

myth is narrative we are given as children
dad waxes poetic   drives through branch brook park
during cherry blossom season   linda's blue muslin dress sleeve
rests on my red wool sweater a planting of sorts
linda and I sing   *you gotta friend*   hand dance in the back
of the chevy   dad turns the radio knob   respect
enter the tunnel of love   kisses required as payment
make wishes to ride forever

　　　　parables teach lessons   soft violence from sweet lips
　　　　fortify those fears of not enough   stories without comfort
　　　　mom's angry tale of a lost red sweater
　　　　her daughter   eejit   queer one
　　　　no more nice things for me   the belt   her calloused hands
　　　　hit hard   my first tattoos   invisible ink of permanent hurt

myth cracks   photo of my kindergarten graduation
buried in a book   kodachrome of 4 children on marble steps
st rose of lima   orange st   blue plaid uniforms
3 white kids to the left   linda in red sweater off to the right
no matter all of dad's urgings   still in the frame
linda sees angelo's angry eyes   like when he beat the dog
angelo told he is everything   white boy
maryanne   the other white girl   glares with rabid jealousy
linda and I fade away from each other   highways claim homes
4th st   7th st   razed to rubble
white flight sweeps the streets   can't say where linda was or is
black lives shattered   seeds of hate scattered

　　　　found picture singes fingers
　　　　linda in the scene   gift from my father
　　　　struggling to rewrite history   failed myth of an ugly lie
　　　　all of us created equal   little girls giving each other gifts
　　　　of sweaters and smiles and songs holding hands
　　　　swaying to music only we can hear
　　　　shame inhabits the distance of so many unhappy endings

Mother

My mother steadied Dad as he stumbled from the car, one hand on his back, the other on his elbow. She whispered to him, out of my earshot, steps behind, as I carried his hat and keys. She eased him onto the bed, gently removed his shoes, propped up the pillows, and softly kissed him on his bald head. "Johnny, you rest." Those hands and whispers and soft kisses transformed into clubs and punches and battering rams where I was concerned. She would beat the Devil out of me, and if He wouldn't leave, as I grew older, she blew the cold wind of hell into us and froze me out.

*

I could see the pure beauty: flaming red hair, porcelain skin, the bluest of the blue eyes, and hands, soft hands, with nails of red to match her hair. I approached without hesitation, drawn to a flame of longing, desire, necessity, comfort, I'm not sure. But once I came within that close proximity where a touch was possible, she changed. It was cold, bitter, the blue of the flame, a destroyer. And her frozen hands iced my heart, still, to this day.

*

It's a shiver in a moment when you would disapprove.
It's a numb finger, the middle one on my right hand
that you chopped off the tip in a door, that pulses with your guilt.
Liquid ice, a biting on my face and the tears fall, a frigid
path down my cheeks.

Bunny Tale

The grey bunny was a Christmas gift from my father,
and I loved him like a friend. At five,
BunnyMan became my first-ever chore.
Food, water, cleaning his cage, grooming, and petting,
we bonded within days. He lived
on our second-floor landing, only
coming inside the apartment
for playtime when mom wasn't home.

The next April on a Sunday morning,
I woke to find the bunny gone.
Mom was at Mass while Dad sat me down
to explain that on the rainy night before,
he met the bunny in a slicker
with Wellingtons and an umbrella,
heading down the backstairs. He was
needed by another little girl and had to leave.
As we dismantled the cage, Dad and I
speculated as to where he was
and how much that little girl
must need him for him to leave me.
We agreed that the time we had together
was special, and even though I was sad,
I would never forget the Bunnyman.

Decades later, as mom slipped into dementia,
she observed the two house buns, Calvin and Hobbes,
as Sarah fed them blueberries on the couch.
Very clinically, she noted that in HER Ireland,
she would have clubbed them over the head,
skinned them, and cooked them for dinner.

There is a place in the heart that will never be filled
—inspired by Charles Bukowski

The bike would wobble,
catch the front wheel
on the uneven pavement

and fall I would,
running to Mom
with blood also running
down my leg:

"No help for that"
as she would turn away
to stare at the kitchen TV,
meat burning
potatoes boiling.

Years later,
you would lie
hooked to monitors,
machines beeping,
"No help for that"
I thought while I waited
for some sign
to save you.

Deck the Halls

Don we now our gay apparel,
Fa la la, la la la, la la la,
Stroll the ancient youthful carol,
Fa la la la la, la la la la.

Set the blazing youth before us,
Fa la la, la la la, la la la,
Strikes the heart and join the circus,
Fa la la la la, la la la la.

My fantastic fall from Catholicism,
committing all of the venial sins
and most of the cardinal ones
(yes, the deadly kind),
perceiving the hymnal revisions
of my pre-pubescent mind
foretold my future rebellions,
flagged by my class leanings.

Raised by a delightful pagan father
and a passionately religious mother,
Irish on both sides,
the pageantry, pomp, and theatrics
of Mass appealed to me,
predicting my devotions to Broadway musicals
and all of Alexander McQueen's oeuvre.
Despite lacking style, quashed by
the daily plaid and knee socks of
the Catholic schoolgirl,
accused by my mother of being a "queer one,"
this was the hymn for me
with its fa's and la's.

I sing it now, noting the words replaced—
troll, Yule, hearth, chorus—
detecting the working-class Vailsburg rhythms
of accents and dialects and patterns
that we wove together unintentionally
to dress the streets with our language—
stroll, youthful, heart, circus—
as we played with abandon,
games made up on the fly,
a parade of colors and countries.
We were so gay
in all the best ways.

Drinking Game

Never have I ever played the game well.
Have you ever skipped school? Been in handcuffs?
Kissed a girl? Boy? Told mom to go to hell?
Got hit? Smoked dope? Fired a gun? Acted tough?
With each tequila sip, as players fell,
chugging their light beer and snacking on stuff,
came questions of darkness; I couldn't tell.
Cheating the sober drinkers, I had enough.

Have you ever lost someone that you love?

The glass sat while my mind wandered
to that empty desk in sixth grade English.
Cancer stole you, no blessings from above,
my first glimpse of death, a young life squandered,
all future losses fail to diminish.

Ode to Pantyhose

Despite my own battles with you,
Pantyhose, with fury and love
I admire your iterations.
Birthed from stockings, which horrified me,
watching my mother hitch them
to the body cast of a girdle,
frantic when they got a run,
to the adding of the pants to the hose,
a concatenation that rendered fear in my heart
yet a bold move toward feminism,
I was forced to wear them
along with a dress on Sunday morning,
making my adolescence even more painful,
uncomfortable in every way at Mass,
cursing the gods under my breath.
In a full liberation maneuver, knee highs
freed me, personally, from further indignity
on my wedding day when I wore
a white gown AND a veil,
a concession to my mother
after she who never cried
cried when I threatened to wear
an Irish lace doily on my head
rather than paying for such a ridiculous item.
I took pleasure in my defiance
when Ken took the garter off my leg,
pushing my dress above my knees
in a display of solidarity
to the delight and dismay of partygoers
and the disdain of my mother.
But, Pantyhose, I fail to jump onboard
this latest bandwagon! The evolution
of leggings—from an undergarment
to casual wear—is too much, even for me.
As Marx predicted, capitalism would consume
itself, my old nemesis, you have stepped out
into a world that will not support your kind.

Divine

Captivated by the meldings of *Cannabalismo*, sitting in my art history class with the aggressively narcissistic professor, either/or-ing his way through a Survey of Modernism, having just watched John Water's *Pink Flamingos*—or the fifth time—I was having no bullshit. The prof's insistence on two-ness embedded in violence (two faceless figures, spoon v. fork, fascism v. socialism, father v. son, right v. left, religion v. economics) left me angry and distant. I had different eyes. Dali's painting and Water's film were both/and's, threats and a trans-gress, movements (dances) into the fragile, ever-morphing in-between.

Divine was my goddess. Heaven and hell didn't exist. Neither did Freud. As the prof droned on, "Sex, cannibalism, and death were linked in Dali's mind," I plunged into the waters of fluidity, willing to drown in glorious uncertainty, weaving together words with no gender, no sex, no religion, no race, no money, words to find other words in a splendid suddenness of serendipity, unpaired, yet familiar, the infatuation of other in all its goodness, like the meltings of Dali and the shit of Water, freed from the binary of everything. Divine is my goddess. I worship nothing.

The History of My Body

Hips like a boy still,
Sixty years in, and muscles
Somewhat firm, my face
The map it is, lines of
Every touch, tenderness.

What This Is Not About

Newark: all my neighborhoods,
Roseville and Vailsburg and Downtown,
out of reach after years away.
Longing for the brick and concrete,
patches of grass and oak trees,
the macadam of the Alexander St. School
playground, where I honed my game,
and Vailsburg Park baseball diamond,
my field of dreams being Willie Mays,
my home the suburbs now.

Parents: Peg and Johnny
don't belong to me anymore.
Mom isn't rationing French Fries
in the Newark College of Engineering
cafeteria, sneaking extra portions onto
the plates of the polite students
who "mind their pleases and thank yous."
Johnny doesn't hold my hand as we
feed the ducks in Branch Brook Park
in the shadow of Sacred Heart Cathedral.

Religion: Irish Catholicism
hung on our walls: crosses,
a portrait of Jesus with a bleeding heart
in our dining room, a cameo
of the Perpetual Heart of Mary
in my parents' bedroom, and
a statue of St. Francis in the vegetable garden,
shyly peeking from behind the rhubarb.
I can still recite my prayers,
but I don't; I write poetry instead.

Longing: all of those losses,
whether the leaving physical or emotional,
or an absence from death,
are holes to be written in,
but not today. Love needs no words
as I brush the toast crumbs from
your mouth between sips of our coffee.

Undressing the World

I pledge allegiance

> red stripes bleeding
> into white

to the flag

> always in the front,
> prominent, dominant,
> my hand clutching my heart
> to quell a pounding panic

of the United States of America

> my father fought for
> my mother left home for

and to the Republic

> that rejects the promise

for which it stands

> to lose its integrity

one nation under God

> breaks His golden rule

indivisible

    slashes our dream

with liberty and justice

    official language
    twists words
    of knowledge and learning

for all

    who look like me

Thank Yous

Undressing the World is dedicated to my father, John B. Lahey, who brought poetry and music and dance, and love to my everyday world and to the city of Newark, New Jersey, my forever landscape. I will always sing your songs. *Is ceol mo chroí thú.*

This book would not exist if not for the love and support of Lynne McEniry who brought me back to the life of a poet and Marina Carreira who believes in Newark and in me. She not only provided invaluable edits on the manuscript but also created the gorgeous cover. *Go raibh maith agat.*

Many of these poems were part of my MFA thesis at Goddard College, written in 1996-1998. I am grateful for the instruction and nurturing of Michael Klein and Nora Mitchell in early versions of some of these poems. In its final iteration, the Write On! Poetry Babes provided feedback, suggestions, and support: Dr. Grisel Y. Acosta, Marina Carreira, Claudia Cortese, Ysabel Gonzalez, Lynne McEniry, PaulA Neves, and Tamara Zhbrizer. *Go raibh maith agat.*

To the places and the people inhabiting those spaces who nourished me: St. Rose of Lima Elementary School (Roseville), Sacred Heart Elementary School (Vailsburg), Marylawn of the Oranges High School (Class of '77), the College of St. Elizabeth (now St. Elizabeth University), Chatham Borough Middle School, West Morris Mendham High School, Goddard College, Drew University, The National SEED Project (Peggy McIntosh and Emily Jane Style), Byrdcliffe Guild Writing Residence, Vermont Studio Center, my Arts By the People family (Paul Rabinowitz), and my Mindful Life meditation family (Jean Vitrano). *Go raibh maith agat.*

To the people who opened their hearts and homes over the years and made their kitchen tables available so these poems could be written: Kristen Ames, Martha Anderson, Sarah Anderson, Shira Brown, Duncan Clegg, Tom Corbo, Bridget Cummings, Mary Cummins, Brenda Derogatis, Dr. Anthony DiBattista, Nancy Ellis,

Michele Fagan, Doug Farrand, Leslie Fry, Wendy Hanks, Kim Helsel, Jean Hughes, Dr. Kathleen Hunter, Sheila Kelleher, Kathy Kremins (the Original), Margaret Lahey, Melissa McHugh, Sean McHugh, Alexander Rosenberg, Bethany Shenise, Franz Vintschger, and Dr. Laura Winters. *Tá croí agat.*

To Finishing Line Press for taking a chance, my editor Christen Kincaid for patiently answering ALL of my questions, Ysabel Gonzalez for the beautiful author photos, and Lynne McEniry, PaulA Neves, and Dimitri Reyes for the generous back cover blurbs. *Go raibh maith agat.*

To Kiera McHugh, Cate McHugh, and Arlo Clegg. I write for you. *Is breá liom tú mo pháiste.*

Kathy Kremins (she/her) is a retired New Jersey public school teacher, coach, and adjunct professor. Born and raised in Newark, NJ, she has a BA from St. Elizabeth University (College of St. Elizabeth), an MFA from Goddard College, and a D. Litt. from Drew University. She is the author of *The Ethics of Reading: The Broken Beauties of Toni Morrison, Arundhati Roy, and Nawal el Sadaawi* (Lambert Academic Publishing, 2010) and an essay contributor to *Too Smart to be Sentimental: Contemporary Irish American Women Writers*. Kathy's recent poems appear in *Soup Can Magazine, The Night Heron Barks, Stay Salty; Life in the Garden State Anthology, Stillwater Review, Lavender Review,* and *Divine Feminist: An Anthology of Poetry & Art By Womxn and Non-Binary Folx*. She is an editor for *NJ Audubon Magazine* and assistant prose editor for *The Platform Review*. She serves as a board member of Arts By the People (ABTP), a non-profit organization whose mission is to establish, operate, promote, and conduct educational programs, opportunities, classes, and sessions in the creative arts for the public, especially seniors and youth. Kathy is also a member of the NJ-based feminist poetry collective Write On! Poetry Babes who read, write, and support all things womxn, queer, trans, and BIPOC. She participates in an ongoing environmental poetry project, Writing the Land (WTL), sponsored by NatureCulture, and two ABTP projects, Bridging Gaps and Intonation that combine poetry, dance, and music. Kathy still lives in New Jersey where she cares for toddler Arlo and pets the chimixes, Elvis and Daphne.

CPSIA information can be obtained
at www.ICGtesting.com
Printed in the USA
BVHW081639060622
639027BV00002B/148

9 781646 628605